AN
In One Day

(2nd Edition)

Y.Ma, The STEM Friend

Copyright © 2023

ISBN: 9798867127305

CONTENTS

THE BASIC II

GREETING

Hi, Nice to meet you!

I am the author of this book. I'm good at many things, like playing video games. Yes, this book is focused on studying, but I would like to talk about playing video games first. Since I am good at video games, for sure I know using strategies can make huge difference. It makes me looks smart when playing video games, and makes other players think they should play in my way. People always say "Do the right things and do things right". We apply this on playing video games, and of course we also can apply this on many other different things, for example learning. Now it is time to come back to our topics.

Did I mention that I also good at math in my second sentence? No? Anyway, we will talk about the American Mathematics Competitions 8 (AMC 8) exam in this book. I would like to show you how we can use different skills and strategies in AMC 8 exam.

How To Use The Book

Before we jump into details of different skills, I will show you how to use this book. You can find "How to use this book" in many other books. But don't skip this one, this is special, short and useful.

We only discuss different skills in this book. We don't have practice questions. Don't worry, it is not a homework book. <u>But after reading each example question, you still can try to solve the problem first, then compare your solution with mine.</u> You may find a better solution other than mine.

After reading this book, you can continue to prepare for the exam, master all necessary knowledge points, or try several practice exams. I also created ten practice tests in another book "AMC 8 Practice Test". First things first, let's finish this book.

2nd Edition

After the first edition was published, I found out that many audiences read super lighting fast. The book cannot cost them one day to finish it. I add more always seen knowledge points. Also update some of those similar problems list.

THE BASIC

The first chapter is always talking about something basic. This book is the same. But people mentioned first thing first. So in this chapter we will look at different skills and strategies, I mean basic skills and strategies. Learning those skills and understanding our strategies can help us doing better in the exam, and, can help us know how to prepare for the exam.

Counting

One, two, three ... before we talk about addition and subtraction, we are going to discuss this very basic mathematical skill — counting. We learn counting before we learned other skills like addition, so I would like to remind you how powerful this basic skill is, and how it can be used in AMC 8 exam. Let's look at some examples.

Problem #1

In grid below, the area of each small square is 1 square inch. What is the combined area of shaded shapes?

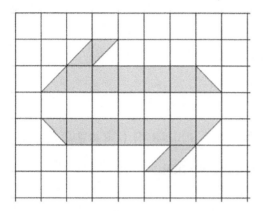

Solution

In the question, we don't have multiple choice ... since we are just talking about counting, we don't need them here.

Look at the diagram, the shapes are made up by many pieces, some squares, and some are only half of a square. Count those half squares like the following, we have one, two, three ... total 8 half squares. That is four full squares. Add to other ten full squares. Then we have fourteen total squares.

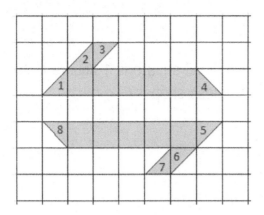

This question mentions that each square is one square inch. So the answer is fourteen square inches.

Problem #2

In following pattern, how many shaded squares are in the fourth diagram?

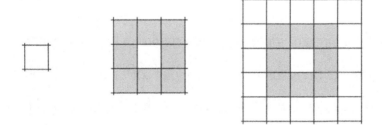

Solution

This problem can be easily solved by drawing out the next diagram in the pattern, then counting the number of shaded squares. The outside layer has twenty four, and the inner layer has eight. In total we have thirty two shaded squares.

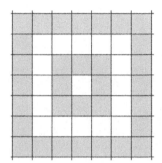 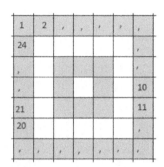

You may notice I write out the numbers when counting. It is not only for explaining purposes. It also shows where we start so we don't accidentally count something twice. When we need to count a large amount, it's easy to forget where we started. So it is good to write out the first several numbers to mark your start point.

Other similar problems

AMC 8 2022 problem 1

AMC 8 2022 problem 4

Drawing

Drawing is a very important skill in math. I am confident that there are many diagrams in your math textbook, like number lines, various charts, coordinate grids and other drawings. Good drawings can help you have a better understanding of the problem, and even can simply it.

Problem #3

A square paper is folded three times as shown below. Then cut a rectangular hole into it.

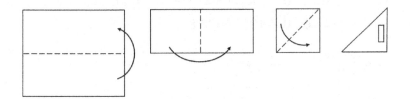

What will the paper look like after it's unfolded?

Solution

This problem can be solved by drawing out the unfolding steps, like shown.

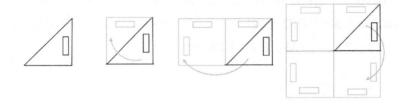

Problem #4

A dice is numbered one through six. The diagram below shows the same dice in three different angles.

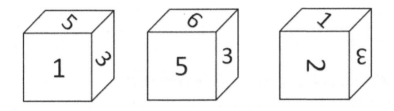

What number is opposite the number five?

Solution

We can see the numbers 1 through 6, with 4 being the only number that cannot be found in the diagram. Can I say the answer is four?

No. Four is not the correct solution. Let's draw it based on the first angle like shown. From the second angle, we can tell six is in the back (opposite side of one). From the third angle, we can tell two is on the bottom (opposite of five). So four is on the left hand side (opposite of three). So, the answer to this problem is two.

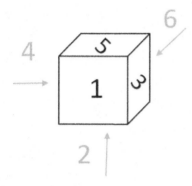

Other similar problems

AMC 8 2022 problem 4

AMC 8 2019 problem 12

Listing

For some math problems, listing out all the possible solutions can be the best way to solve them. Especially for those problems that have small numbers.

Problem #5

Three different positive integers a, b and c. Given that a > b > c, and their product is 90. In how many ways can the numbers be chosen?

(A) 4   (B) 5   (C) 6   (D) 7   (E) 8

Solution

This question sounds like a question about factors and possibility. 90 for 3 different positive integers multiplication, how many possible ways are there? Let's look at those choices — all small numbers. Maybe we can list them all.

First, let's start from a small number. So list possible values for number 'c'. It can be 1, 2, 3, 5, 9, 10 ... wait! 10 is too big for the smallest number, since we also need to multiply

14

two bigger numbers to get 90. Same goes for 5 and 9. So 'c' can be 1, 2, or 3.

When 'c' is 3, then $a \times b = 30$, that is 5×6. One way.

When 'c' is 2, then $a \times b = 45$, they can be 3×15, 5×9. Two ways.

When 'c' is 1, then $a \times b = 90$, available values for number 'b' are: 2, 3, 5, 6, 9. Five ways.

So there are totally $1 + 2 + 5 = [E]$ 8 ways.

Problem #6

A pizza store cooks one pizza every five minutes, and sells one slice (an eighth of a pizza) every 30 seconds. When the store opens, there are two whole pizzas already cooked. How many minutes later, the store will run out of pizzas to sell?

(A) 8   (B) 21   (C) 24   (D) 25   (E) 28

Solution

List all times for cooking and selling pizzas as following. It takes four minutes to sell one pizza, so eight minutes to sell those two existing pizzas at the beginning. But at five minutes, the third pizza is ready. Then at twelve minutes we sold that pizza. But at ten minutes we have the fourth pizza ready. Continue those steps, we can see at twenty four minutes we sold the sixth pizza, but next pizza is not ready yet. So the answer is [C] : twenty four minutes.

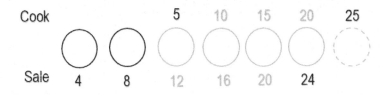

Other similar problems

AMC 8 2022 problem 3

AMC 8 2022 problem 22

Calculations

Now let's talk about addition and subtraction, I mean those basic operations we learn in school. AMC 8 exams have questions for different levels, from easy to not so easy. So don't be surprised when you see some AMC 8 questions just as easy as those in your math textbook.

Problem #7

John plans to read an eight hundred page book. On the first day, he read two hundred pages. On the second day, he read one half of those remaining pages. The same thing happened on the third and fourth days. How many pages have been read by the end of fourth day?

(A) 200   (B) 400   (C) 600   (D) 725   (E) 800

Solution

After first day, John has eight hundred minus two hundred equals six hundred pages left.

On day two, John read six hundred divided by two equals three hundred pages left.

On day three, he read three hundred divided by two equals one hundred and fifty pages, which means he has one hundred and fifty pages left to read.

Finally, John read one hundred and fifty divide by two equals seventy five pages, and has seventy five pages left. During the four days, John read eight hundred minus seventy five equals seven hundred and twenty five pages.

The answer is [D] : seven hundred and twenty five pages read.

Problem #8

Which of the following expressions has the largest value?

(A) $3 + 2 + 1 + 0$

(B) $3 \times 2 + 1 + 0$

(C) $3 + 2 \times 1 + 0$

(D) $3 + 2 + 1 \times 0$

(E) $3 \times 2 \times 1 \times 0$

Solution

Expression (A) is equal to six

Expression (B) is equal to seven

Expression (C) is equal to five

Expression (D) is equal to five

Expression (E) is equal to zero

Seven is that largest value, so the answer is [B].

Other similar problems

AMC 8 2022 problem 9

AMC 8 2017 problem 1

Trial and Error

There is a type of AMC 8 problems that is designed to look super hard. You can even tell that no one can solve them in time. Don't give up yet. Those questions are made to be solved by students like you who take the exam. Try to play with it for a bit. You might immediately find the trick, and solve the problem. Let's look at some examples to check how important it is to try before you give up and guess.

Problem #9

What is the value of the units digit of 3^{1234}?

(A) 1 (B) 3 (C) 5 (D) 7 (E) 9

Solution

Three to the power of one thousand two hundred and thirty four is equal to three times three times three ...(total of one thousand two hundred and thirty four "three"s). No one can finish it in time. And I don't have any other way of solving it at a glance. But let's try.

Three times three equals nine, nine times three is twenty seven (unit digit of seven, so we can ignore the twenty), seven times three is twenty one (units digit of one, so again we can ignore the twenty)

Something interesting here. The problem is asking for unit digit, and we found a list of units digits, in order from three, nine, seven, one. Because one times three equals three, we know that this is a four term repeating pattern.

One thousand two hundred and thirty four divided by four (the number of terms in the pattern) is three hundred and eight with a remainder of two. Because there is a remainder of two, we can count two terms from the pattern. So three to the power of one thousand two hundred and thirty three is three (first term of the pattern), and three to the power of one thousand two hundred and thirty four would be nine (second term of the pattern).

So the answer to this problem would be [E] : 9.

Problem #10

What is the value of the following expression?

$$(1 - \frac{1}{2}) \times (1 - \frac{1}{3}) \times (1 - \frac{1}{4}) \times \ldots \times (1 - \frac{1}{99})$$

(A) 0 (B) $\frac{35}{99}$ (C) $\frac{1}{99}$ (D) $\frac{93672}{3476851}$ (E) $\frac{27639}{3476851}$

Solution

This problem looks complicated, and it need a very long time to do the math. But let's play with it first.

$$(1 - \frac{1}{2}) = \frac{1}{2}$$

$$(1 - \frac{1}{3}) = \frac{2}{3}$$

$$(1 - \frac{1}{4}) = \frac{3}{4}$$

...

$$(1 - \frac{1}{2}) \times (1 - \frac{1}{3}) \times (1 - \frac{1}{4}) \times \ldots \times (1 - \frac{1}{99}) = \frac{1}{2} \times \frac{2}{3} \times \frac{3}{4} \times \ldots \times \frac{98}{99}$$

Looks like we found the solution, we can cancel fractions like shown.

$$\frac{1}{\cancel{2}} \times \frac{\cancel{2}}{\cancel{3}} \times \frac{\cancel{3}}{\cancel{4}} \times \ldots \times \frac{\cancel{98}}{99} = \frac{1}{99}$$

So the answer is [C] : $\dfrac{1}{99}$

Other similar problems

AMC 8 2022 problem 8

AMC 8 2022 problem 17

Process of Elimination

When working on multiple choice questions, we have to mention the method of eliminating incorrect options. In fact, crossing out those wrong options can be the only good solution for some AMC 8 questions. Usually, based on our understanding of the problem, we use one or multiple conditions to examine each choice, and cross out incorrect ones, until we got the correct one.

This method has a simplified version — try those options one by one. When the problem is simple enough, we can check those options one by one until we find the correct solution.

Problem #11

For two positive integers A and B, A is four times the value of B, and average of A and B is fifteen. What is the value of B?

(A) 4   (B) 5   (C) 6   (D) 7   (E) 8

Solution

Try (A), four times four equals sixteen, sixteen plus four is twenty, twenty divided by two is ten, incorrect.

Try (B), four times five equals twenty, twenty plus five equals twenty five, twenty five divided by two is twelve and a half, incorrect.

Try (C), four times six equals twenty four, twenty four plus six is thirty, thirty divide by two is fifteen , which is the correct answer.

You already have the answer, checking (D) and (E) are optional. When you have enough time in the exam, for example you already finished all problems, review and check your answers. We can check (D) and (E) to make sure (C) is the only correct one.

Try (D), four times seven is twenty eight, twenty eight plus seven is thirty five, and thirty five divided by two equals seventeen and a half, incorrect.

Try (E), four times eight equals thirty two, thirty tow plus eight is forty, and forty divided by two equals twenty, incorrect.

For this question, if you are good at math, it also can be solved easily like the following. So the formal solution can be:

Let x be the value of the integer B.

$$(x \times 4 + x) \div 2 = 15$$

$$(5x) \div 2 = 15$$

$$5x = 30$$

$$x = 6$$

In previous question, we have other solutions. So we use this method only when it is easy to use — small numbers, easy calculations, or we forget that we can use math equations to solve the problem. But in many cases, crossing out incorrect one is the best solution. Please refer to next problem for example.

Keep in mind that we can apply different conditions to check those options. If after using one condition, we have more than one options leave, we can use other conditions, until we find the correct one.

Problem #12

Mary ran at consistent speed for four miles, then rests for one hour. After the rest she continue to run for one hour in the same speed. Which of following diagram shows miles Marcy run over time?

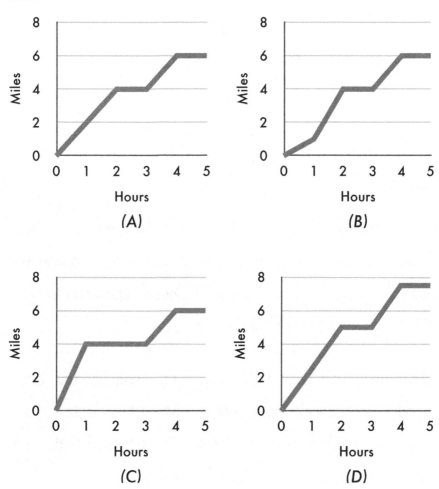

(A)

(B)

(C)

(D)

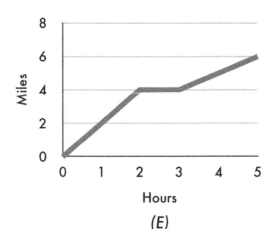

(E)

Solution

Let's follow the story, and check these diagrams one by one. "Mary run at consistent speed for four miles", option (B) doesn't show consistent speed, (D) doesn't show run for four miles, so we can cross out (B) and (D).

We have (A), (C) and (E) left. Let's continue, use other conditions to check those options. "Mary then rests for one hour". (A) is ok. (C) is not, it shows two hours of rest. (E) is fine. We cross out (C), still have (A) or (E).

If we run out of conditions, we may do a reasonable guessing here. But the story not finished yet, we can look into other conditions. "After that Mary run for one hour in the same speed", (E) doesn't show run for one hour, also doesn't show run at same speed. Cross out (E).

So the only correct options is [A]

Other similar problems

AMC 8 2022 problem 6

AMC 8 2022 problem 10

Reading Carefully

We must read the question carefully. Otherwise ... not only can we choose the wrong answer, but it also can make us use more time. Let's say you find the result after a calculation, but none of those options fit for your result. One reason is that you made mistake when calculating. Also, you may have misread or misunderstood the problem. That cost us more time to finish the problem. Remember, AMC 8 is a timed test.

Also, wrong results are most of the answer choices. They carefully pick incorrect answers in an effort to trick you.

Problem #13

Alex walk eighteen hundred meters in constant speed. He walks three steps per two seconds, and one meter per two steps. How many minutes does he need to walk the distance?

(A) 20   (B) 40   (C) 60   (D) 2400   (E) 3000

Solution

Alex walks one meter per two steps, three steps per two seconds. So he walks three meters per four seconds (six steps).

To finish the walking, he needs eighteen hundred divided by three fourths equals six hundred times four equals twenty four hundred seconds.

So the answer is (D) ? No, incorrect. The problem is asking for how many minutes, so the answer is twenty four hundred divided by sixty equals forty minutes. So the answer is [B] : 40

Problem #14

Students in Ms. Bella's class record the number of minutes they spend reading each day. The following diagram shows how many minutes they read yesterday. What's the average number of minutes they read yesterday?

(A) 25   (B) 27.5   (C) 28   (D) 29   (E) 30

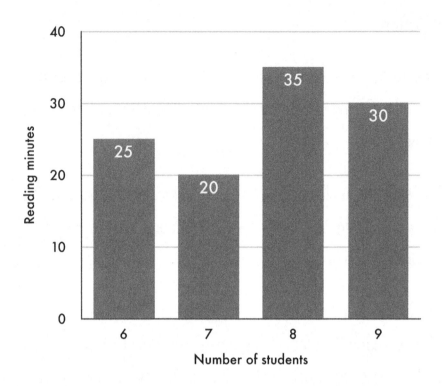

Solution

This problem asking for average minutes. Twenty five plus twenty plus thirty five equals four hundred and forty, four hundred and forty divided by four is one hundred and ten, one hundred and ten divided by four is twenty seven and a half.

So the answer is (B)? No, (B) is incorrect. There are six students that read for twenty five minutes, seven students that read for twenty minutes, eight students that read for thirty five minutes and nine students that read for thirty minutes.

$$(25 \times 6 + 20 \times 7 + 35 \times 8 + 30 \times 9) \div (6 + 7 + 8 + 9)$$

$$= (150 + 140 + 280 + 270) \div 30$$

$$= 840 \div 30$$

$$= 28. \text{ The answer is } [C]$$

Other similar problems

AMC 8 2022 problem 7

AMC 8 2018 problem 8

Reasonable Guessing

It is quite normal that in during an exam we are not able to find the correct answer for a question. Can we do anything in those situations? Yes, we can guess the answer. This is because the AMC 8 exam has no wrong answer penalty. That means that there will be no points deducted if you get an answer wrong, but you won't get any either.

In addition, after we apply the process of elimination, we can increase our chance to guess the correct answer.

Let's pretend we are working on the last problem of a AMC 8 exam. We don't have enough time. But we are lucky enough, the last question is super easy for REASONABLE guessing.

Problem #15

As shown in the following diagram, there is a square between the two circles that have same center point. Which fraction is closest to the ratio of shaded area to the area between two circles?

(A) $\dfrac{1}{3}$ (B) 1 (C) $\dfrac{5}{4}$ (D) 2 (E) $\dfrac{5}{2}$

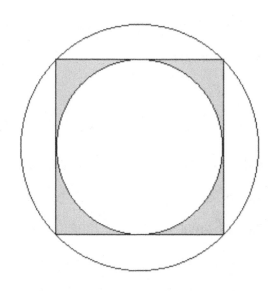

Solution

Since we are running low on time, lets randomly guess, (C) is the answer. But what is our reasoning? We are talking about reasonable guessing. Ok, let's do it again.

We are finding the ratio of the shaded area and area of the ring. And look at those options. (A) is the best option for guessing. The shaded area is smaller than the ringed area. (A) is the only one smaller than one. The question is asking for the closest fraction, and there is still a chance for the answer to be (B). Look at the diagram again, it is most likely to be (A) than (B).

Comparing it to our previously randomly picked answer (C), don't you think (A) is more reasonable?

What is the correct solution for this problem, if we have enough time and don't guess at all? In fact, it is not that difficult. Let's say the radius of small circle is r, then the area of the small circle is πr^2.

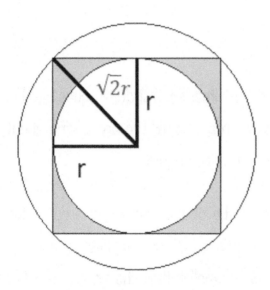

The side length of the square is 2r, then the area of the square is $4r^2$

Radius of the large circle is $\sqrt{r^2 + r^2} = \sqrt{2r^2} = \sqrt{2} \cdot r$, then the area of the large circle is $2\pi r^2$

So the ratio of shaded area to the ring area is
$$\frac{4r^2 - \pi r^2}{2\pi r^2 - \pi r^2} = \frac{(4 - \pi)r^2}{\pi r^2} = \frac{4 - \pi}{\pi}$$

Let's say π is about 3.14 then the ratio is about 0.27. Answer (A) is the closest to it.

Problem #16

Draw a square within following shape. What is the largest area the square can have?

(A) 100   (B) 110   (C) 120   (D) 130   (E)140

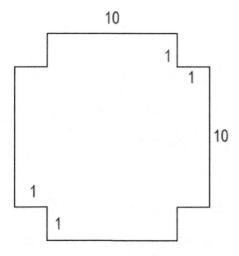

Solution

Let's see what we know for now. If we draw the square like this, the area will be (A), one hundred.

But if we tilt it a little bit, it can be bigger. Like following. What is the area of this square?

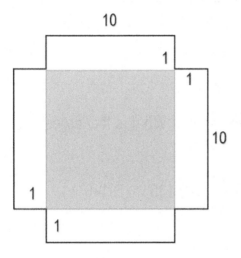

(A) is not the correct one, we now know, the result should be larger than this. The area of the whole shape is $(12 \times 12) - 4 \times (1 \times 1) = 144 - 4 = 140$. So, (E) is incorrect. If you are not able to solve this problem during the exam, let us do reasonable guessing. Look at our drawing again, I would choose the answer (C), one hundred and twenty, which is the average of one hundred and one hundred and forty.

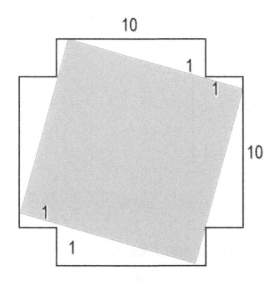

Now, let's take a look on the solution. Refer to following diagram. The area of the large square is equal to the area of the small square plus area of the four triangles. Looking closely at area of these triangles, we find that the area of $\triangle EBC$ is equal to half the area of the rectangle ABCD. $\triangle ABE = \triangle BEF$, and $\triangle CDE = \triangle CEF$.

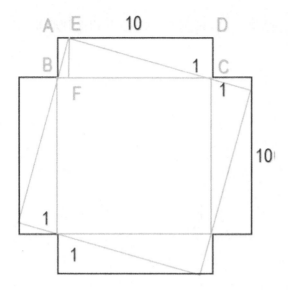

The area of the small square is one hundred, the area of whole shape is one hundred and forty. So the area of the four rectangles is forty, then for each rectangle. The area of the four triangles is five each, twenty in total. So, the large square has an area of one hundred plus twenty equals one hundred and twenty. So the answer is [C].

Other similar problems

AMC 8 2015 problem 25

AMC 8 2011 problem 25

Don't Slow Down

Hurry up! Speed, speed, speed!

Read carefully doesn't mean we can do it slowly. Instead, during the exam we must keep our speed. This is the most essential point I would like you to remember.

I keep saying that the AMC 8 exam is not difficult at all. But why is it that not all the students get high scores on the exam? The reason is we only have forty minutes to finish twenty five questions. As a middle school student, you have taken many tests before. But you might not realize what is so special about the setting at a glance. The special thing is that the exam isn't like other tests in school, which are just designed to make sure we know the knowledge points in the textbook. Even the best students can feel trapped and stumped by one or two questions during the exam. In average we have ninety six seconds for each question, and those confusing questions need more time. We can't waste any time during the exam. So, never slow down!

Let's plan ahead on what strategy we will use for the AMC 8 exam. Plan one minute for each question, using up twenty five minutes. There can be one or two questions that need more time, for example three minutes. So we can leave about ten minutes to check our answers, or work on those problems that are not yet done. Based on this idea, we can skip questions that we don't have any idea yet. We randomly give an answer for that question, and mark the question as one that we guessed. We can come back to the question later after we finish other questions we know.

Now we have our strategy for the exam. How good will they work in the exam? You can try a practice exam, find real AMC 8 exam questions from past years, and try to finish those questions in forty minutes.

Be Patient

Believe or not, once or twice we may see AMC 8 includes questions that require us to be patient. When facing this kind of problem, taking it step by step is the best solution. But don't believe that all problems fall into this category. Remember what we discussed earlier, don't slow down. So if a question is too time consuming, we can skip to the next one and come back to it later.

Problem #17

There is a 🐷 button on a funny calculator. If a number on the screen is no more than 50, it will add 6 to the number. If the number on the screen is equal to or more than 50, it will subtract 50 from the number. The screen shows 10 at the beginning. At least how many times we need to press the 🐷 button to make the screen show 0?

(A) 10   (B) 14   (C) 16   (D) 17   (E) 18

Solution

We just need to list out all the results in every steps like the following to find the answer.

	1st	2nd	3rd	4th	5th	6th	7th	8th	9th	10th
10	16	22	28	34	40	46	52	2	8	14
	11th	12th	13th	14th	15th	16th	17th			
	20	26	32	38	44	50	0			

The answer is (E).

Problem #18

There are 2 bacterias in the petri dish. Every hour, the number of bacterias will double. After how many hours, the number of bacterias will be more than 1000?

(A) 8   (B) 9   (C) 10   (D) 11   (E)20

Solution

We just need to list out all the results in every hours like the following to find the answer.

1st	2nd	3rd	4th	5th	6th	7th	8th	9th
4	8	16	32	64	128	256	512	1024

The answer is (B).

Other similar problems

AMC 8 2022 problem 22

AMC 8 2023 problem 4

THE BASIC II

I agree that this chapter title sounds a little bit … lazy. When writing this chapter, it comes into my mind. It makes sense to me in some ways. It emphasizes the AMC 8 exam is not difficult, and it tests those basic math knowledge points we learn. In the first part, we discussed some basic skills that can be used on the exam. This chapter, we are going to discuss several basic knowledge points in this chapter.

In order to keep this book short, to make the book possible for readers to finish it within one day, it is impossible to cover too many knowledge points here. We are going to only discuss several topics in this chapter.

Operations

It is quite normal to define a new operation with existing operation(s) in math. For example, multiplication can be defined using addition. $8 \times 9 = 8 + 8 + \ldots + 8$ (totally nine eights added up together). When we understand this idea, we start to understand what they are talking about when it come to problems defining a nonexistent operation.

Problem #19

Let's say a || b = $\dfrac{a + b}{a - b}$, what is the value of 10 || 8?

(A) 0   (B) 1   (C) 8   (D) 9   (E) 10

Solution

In order to get 10 || 8, we apply 'a' = 10 and 'b' = 8 to following expression (replace 'a' with ten, replace 'b' with eight).

$$\frac{a+b}{a-b} = \frac{10+8}{10-8}.$$

Then calculate the result, $\dfrac{10+8}{10-8} = \dfrac{18}{2} = 9.$

The answer is [D]

Problem #20

If a 🚲 b = a - b x 0.1, what is the value of ((0.8 🚲 2) 🚲 3)?

(A) 0.1   (B) 0.3   (C) 0.5   (D) 0.7   (E) 0.9

Solution

First calculate $(0.8 \text{ 🚲 } 2) = (0.8 - 2 \times 0.1) = 0.6$, next $(0.6 \text{ 🚲 } 3) = (0.6 - 3 \times 0.1) = 0.3$, the answer is [B]

Other similar problems

AMC 8 2022 problem 2

AMC 8 2022 problem 17

Formulas

Similar to the new operations, we can also see some "physical formulas" in the exam. Don't worry, this is a math test, not a physics test. In fact, these formulas can be made-up, but we don't care, we just need to plug those numbers into the formula to get the result.

However, they do expect us to understand one physics formula, the speed formula, $D = v \times t$. Distance(D) is equal to speed(v) times time(t). Of course, this formula can also have two other forms, $v = \dfrac{D}{t}$ and $t = \dfrac{D}{v}$.

Problem #21

A bucket contains 20 inches deep water. The formula below is used to calculate the new water level after putting a ball into it. In the formula, "Original" is the original height of water in the bucket, "Weight" is the weight of the ball dropped into the bucket, and "Height" will be the new height of water in the bucket. What will be the new water level after dropping one 0.56 pound ball into the bucket?

(A) 20.08   (B) 20.1   (C) 20.8   (D) 21   (E) 28

$$Height = Original + Weight \div 0.7$$

Solution

We just need to plug those number into the formula.

$$Height = Original + Weight \div 0.7 = 20 + 0.56 \div 0.7 = 20 + 0.8 = 20.8$$

The answer is [C].

Problem #22

Karl walks 1 mile to school. He leaves home at the same time each day, walks at a speed of 2 miles per hour. Today he walked the first 1/2 mile as usual. Then he spent 3 minutes and bought an ice cream. At how many miles per hour must Karl walk the last 1/2 mile in order to arrive school as his usual time?

(A) 2.1   (B) 2.2   (C) 2.3   (D) 2.4   (E) 2.5

Solution

Karl walks 30 minutes on a usual day. Today he walks 15 minutes for the first half mile. The second half mile, he needs to finish in $15 - 3 = 12$ minutes. Apply the speed formula, we know Karl's speed for the second half is equal to $v = \dfrac{D}{t} = \dfrac{1}{2} \div \dfrac{12}{60} = \dfrac{1}{2} \times \dfrac{60}{12} = \dfrac{5}{2}$ mph. The answer is [E].

Other similar problems

AMC 8 2023 problem 3

AMC 8 2023 problem 15

Prime Numbers

Prime numbers are those positive integers who have two factors, one and itself. For example, seven has only two factors, one and seven. Since the number one only has one factor, it doesn't count as a prime number. Prime numbers start from two. Two is very special, it is the only even prime number.

Many other topics can be extended from prime numbers. For example, prime factorization, GCF, LCM, fraction calculation, etc. Also, those can be used combining with other knowledge to create many interesting questions.

Problem #23

How many factors of 90 has at least four factors?

(A) 1   (B) 6   (C) 7   (D) 8   (E) 11

Solution

Do prime factorization for ninety, we know $90 = 2 \times 3^2 \times 5$

If a factor of ninety is a product of two different prime numbers, for example $6 = 2 \times 3$, it has four factors: one, two, three, and six. Based on this, we can list out all those factors of ninety, and have four or more factors as following.

Use two prime numbers: $2 \times 3 = 6$, $2 \times 5 = 10$ and $3 \times 5 = 15$. Notice that 3×3 is not valid, nine only has three factors, we need two different prime numbers.

Use three prime numbers: $3 \times 3 \times 5 = 45$ (excluding the 2), $2 \times 3 \times 5 = 30$ (excluding one 3), $2 \times 3 \times 3 = 18$ (excluding the 5);

Four of those prime numbers: $2 \times 3 \times 3 \times 5 = 90$

So there are totally seven factors has at least four factors: six, ten, fifteen, eighteen, thirty, forty five, and ninety. Other factors of ninety have no more than three factors: one, two, three, five, and nine. The answer is [C] 7.

Problem #24

In a bag of marbles, one third are red, two fifths are blue, and five marbles are green. No more than six marbles are yellow. How many yellow marbles in the bag?

(A) 1   (B) 2   (C) 3   (D) 4   (E) 5

Solution

Let's say there are totally N marbles in the bag. Since one third of the marbles are red, two fifths of the marbles are blue, N is a multiple of three and five. That is $N = 3 \times 5 \times x = 15 \times x$, multiple of fifteen.

Lets verify N=15. $15 \times \dfrac{1}{3} = 5$ red marbles. $15 \times \dfrac{2}{5} = 6$ blue marbles. Four marbles left, but it said there are five green marbles. So, N=15 incorrect.

Let's try N=30. $30 \times \dfrac{1}{3} = 10$ red marbles. $30 \times \dfrac{2}{5} = 12$ blue marbles. Five green marbles. $30 - 10 - 12 - 5 = 3$ yellow marbles, less than six. This one valid.

The answer is [C].

Can it be N=45? Doing the same calculations, we get fifteen red marbles, eighteen blue marbles, five green marbles and seven brown marbles, which is more than. six. N=45 incorrect

Other similar problems

AMC 8 2020 problem 17

AMC 8 2019 problem 23

Average

Average is a basic concept, so of course it will be included on some AMC 8 exams. Besides that, if we use that correctly, it can help us save time.

Problem #25

The sum of 10 consecutive even integers is 210. What is the largest one of these 10 integers?

(A) 22   (B) 24   (C) 26   (D) 28   (E) 30

Solution

The sum of ten even numbers is 210, the average is 21. So the fifth and sixth numbers are 20 and 22. Count it, 22, 24, 26, 28, 30. The answer is (E).

Problem #26

Terry competes in a three-day bike race. He rode 55 miles a day. On the first day, he finished the race in 3 hours and 30 minutes. The next day, he spent 4 hours. How long will it take

Terry to complete his final day of riding so that his 3-day average speed is 15 mph?

(A) 3 hours and 30 minutes   (B) 3 hours and 45 minutes

(C) 4 hours   (D) 4 hours and 15 minutes

(E) 4 hours and 30 minutes

Solution

The target average speed is 15 mph, the total distance is 55x3=165 miles, so the total time should be 165/15=11 hours. 11-7.5=3.5 hours. The answer is [A].

Other similar problems

AMC 8 2022 problem 2

AMC 8 2019 problem 16

Data Set

Venn diagrams are very useful when solving problems about sets. For example, the diagram below shows that some customers ordered pizza in the store, some customers ordered apple juice, and some customers ordered both.

Pizza

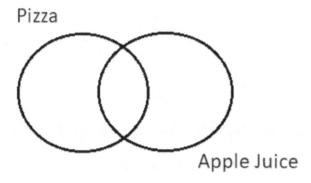

Apple Juice

Sometimes, for simple enough questions, listing out all the information in a table also can help.

Problem #27

There are 22 customers in a restaurant. 13 people ordered apple juice, 17 customers ordered pizza. At least how many customers ordered pizza together with apple juice?

(A) 8   (B) 9   (C) 10   (D) 11   (E) 12

Solution

The problem asks at least how many customers ordered pizza with apple juice. We had $22 - 17 = 5$ customers who didn't order pizza. Let's assume they all order apple juice, so that we have as few as possible customers order pizza with apple juice. That is $13 - 5 = 8$. The answer is [A].

Problem #28

There are 13 girls and 12 boys in Mr. Bob's class. 48% of them chose math as their favorite subject, and 52% chose ELS. However, 2/3 of boys choose maths as their favorite subject. How many girls in the class chose ELA as their favorite subject?

(A) 4   (B) 5   (C) 7   (D) 9   (E) 11

Solution

We list out everything as the following. First, we calculate to know there are 25 students. Next, we know there are 13 students chose ELA. Then, we know there are 8 boys chose math and 4 boys chose ELA. So we know 9 girls chose ELA. The answer is [D].

	13 girls	12 boys	25 students
Math		$12 \times \dfrac{2}{3} = 8$	$25 \times 48\% = 12$
ELA	$13 - 4 = 9$	$12 - 8 = 4$	$25 \times 52\% = 13$

Other similar problems

AMC 8 2019 problem 11

AMC 8 2019 problem 15

Sequence

Sequence is a group of numbers. We know the mean, the median, the mode and the range of a sequence. There is a special type of sequence called arithmetic sequence. It is just like we do skip-counting. If we know the first number, know the gap (how many we skip), we can calculate any number in a given position. Also, we know how to make a pair to calculate the sum of an arithmetic sequence.

$$Sum = (First + Last) \times \frac{Counts}{2}$$

Problem #29

Helen began to read a book. She plans to read 20 pages on Monday. For the next few days, she would read five more pages each day than she did the day before. In this way she can read the book in 7 days. How many pages are there in this book?

(A) 105   (B) 140   (C) 170   (D) 220   (E) 245

Solution

The first day Helen read 20 pages, the next day she read 25 pages, the third day she read 30 pages, and so on. The seventh day, she read $20 + (7 - 1) \times 5 = 50$ pages. So we can calculate the pages of book, $(20 + 50) \times \dfrac{7}{2} = 245$. The answer is [E].

Other similar problems

AMC 8 2023 problem 20

AMC 8 2022 problem 19

Possibility

In math, possibility means how great the chance something will happen. Usually we count the number of possible results we want, then divide it by the number of all possible results. The answer is between zero and one. This topic not only includes possibility calculations, but also the counting method.

Problem #30

How many even numbers with distinct digits are larger than 1999 and smaller than 8999?

(A) 1500   (B) 1736   (C) 1960   (D) 3500   (E) 7000

Solution

We can solve this problem by following steps.

Step One: Choose one digit for the unit digit, we can pick from zero, two, four, six, eight. Totally five choices

Step Two: Choose value for the thousands digit. In this step, we need to consider what we pick on step one. If in step one we picked zero, in step two we can pick from one to eight. If in step one we pick other choices, we can pick from zero to eight, except the one we picked in step one. For example, if we picked six for unit digit, we can pick two, three, four, five, seven, or, eight. We can't chose six for the thousands digit.

Step Three: Choose value for the hundreds digit. In step one and two, we picked two different digits already, in this step we can pick from other eight digits

Step Four: Choose value for the tens digit. In other steps we picked three different digits already, in this step we can pick from other seven digits

So for those numbers - - - 0, we have $7 \times 8 \times 7 = 392$ different numbers. For those numbers that end with two, four, six, or eight, we have $4 \times 6 \times 8 \times 7 = 1344$. In total, there are one thousand seven hundred and thirty six numbers that fit the conditions in the problem.

So the answer is [B].

Problem #31

In a bag, there are one red marble, two blue marbles, three green marbles, and four yellow marbles. One at a time, a marble is take out from the bag randomly. The marble will not be put back to the bag. What is the chance of the third marble to be taken out from the bag to be blue?

(A) $\dfrac{1}{8}$ (B) $\dfrac{1}{5}$ (C) $\dfrac{1}{4}$ (D) $\dfrac{8}{21}$ (E) $\dfrac{25}{72}$

Solution

Since we don't know what the first marble and second marble are, we can take out three marbles A, B, C, put them together, and see what color is C. It will be not different than if I just took out C, and take out A and B later. So we have a $\dfrac{2}{10}$ chance that the third marble is blue. Answer is [B].

Let's try another way, do it following the steps described in the problem. First we take out the first marble.

Blue $\dfrac{2}{10}$ Others $\dfrac{8}{10}$

Then take the second marble.

If first marble is blue, for the second one: Blue
$\frac{2}{10} \times \frac{1}{9} = \frac{2}{90}$ Others $\frac{2}{10} \times \frac{8}{9} = \frac{16}{90}$

If first marble is not blue, for the second one: Blue
$\frac{8}{10} \times \frac{2}{9} = \frac{16}{90}$ Others $\frac{8}{10} \times \frac{7}{9} = \frac{56}{90}$

So after taking out the two marbles, there is a $\frac{2}{90}$ chance for two blue marbles are taken out, a $(\frac{16}{90} + \frac{16}{90})$ chance only one blue marble is taken out, and a $\frac{56}{90}$ chance all blue marbles are still in the bag. When it comes to third marble, chance of drawing out a blue one is

$$\frac{2}{90} \times 0 + (\frac{16}{90} + \frac{16}{90}) \times \frac{1}{8} + \frac{56}{90} \times \frac{2}{8} = 0 + \frac{32}{90 \times 8} + \frac{112}{90 \times 8} = \frac{144}{90 \times 8} = \frac{1}{5}$$

So the answer is again, [B]

Other similar problems

AMC 8 2022 problem 14

AMC 8 2022 problem 25

Algebra - Equation

Algebra is a powerful but difficult method we should master to solve problems. We use variables (for example x, y, and z) to replace known or unknown numbers, then list out equations. Then find values for those variables by solving the equation(s).

Problem #32

One quarter of the sixth graders are in the math club. Two fifths of the seventh graders are in the math club. There are an equal number of sixth graders and seventh graders in the club. What is the ratio of sixth graders to seventh graders?

(A) 2:1   (B) 4:5   (C) 8:5   (D) 5:8   (E) 1:2

Solution

Suppose there are X students in the sixth grade and Y students in the seventh grade. So we can write the equation:

$$\frac{1}{4}X = \frac{2}{5}Y$$

So, $5X = 4 \times 2Y$

$5X = 8Y$

We are looking for X:Y, or $\dfrac{X}{Y}$.

From the equation, we have $\dfrac{X}{Y} = \dfrac{8}{5}$.

Answer is [C]

Problem #33

In a bag, we have seven red marbles, eight blue marbles, and nine yellow marbles. After adding some blue marbles into the bag, fifty percent marbles are now blue. How many blue marbles were added into the bag?

(A) 5　(B) 6　(C) 7　(D) 8　(E) 9

Solution

Let's say there are X blue marbles are added into the bag. We can write out the equation like following.

$$\frac{8+x}{7+8+9+x} = 50\%$$

So, $\dfrac{8+x}{24+x} = \dfrac{1}{2}$

$$24 + x = 2 \times (8 + x)$$

$$24 + x = 16 + 2x$$

$$x = 8$$

Answer is [D].

Other similar problems

AMC 8 2022 problem 6

AMC 8 2023 problem 13

Geometry - Circle

Circles are a popular geometry test point on the AMC 8 exam. This must be learned. The good news is that those knowledge are fun and easy to remember. For example, the distance from the center of a circle to any point on the circle is the same - it is the radius; the formula for the area is πr^2; the formula for the perimeter is $2\pi r$; the most interesting thing is that the diameter forms a right triangle with any point on the circle; also many other fun facts about circles.

Problem #34

As show in following diagram, right triangle $\triangle ABC$ is inscribed in a semicircle with radius five. Length of AB is eight. What is the length of BC?
(A) 4   (B) 4.8   (C) 5   (D) 6.3   (E) 8

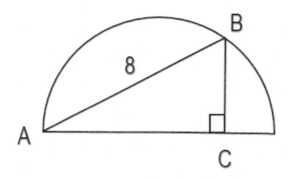

Solution

Add line segment BD as following. It is a semicircle, so triangle $\triangle ABD$ is right triangle.

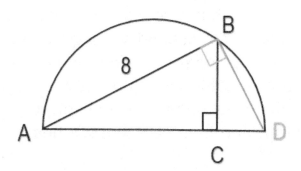

Length of AD is $5 \times 2 = 10$, so length of BD is $\sqrt{10^2 - 8^2} = \sqrt{100 - 64} = \sqrt{36} = 6$.

Area of triangle $\triangle ABD$ can be calculated by $\dfrac{AB \times BD}{2}$ or $\dfrac{AD \times BC}{2}$. So length of BC is $\dfrac{8 \times 6}{10} = 4.8$

So, the answer is [B].

Other similar problems

AMC 8 2020 problem 18

AMC 8 2023 problem 12

Geometry - Similar Triangle

While circles are interesting, similar triangles are tricky. When talking about similar triangles, immediately we remember that similar triangles have the same shape but size can be different. They have the same corresponding angles, and have the same ratio of corresponding sides. The ratio of their area is equal to the square of the ratio of their side. But the tricky part is how to know if two triangles are similar, and then how that will help us solve the problem.

Problem #35

As shown in the figure below, CDEF is a square. Length of $\overline{AC}$ is 2. Length of $\overline{BC}$ is 3. What is the length of $\overline{DE}$?
(A) 1   (B) 1.2   (C) 1.5   (D) 1.8   (E) 2

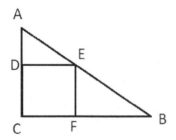

Solution

Notice that $\triangle ADE$, $\triangle EFB$, and $\triangle ABC$ are similar triangles. So we have $\overline{AD} : \overline{DE} = \overline{EF} : \overline{BF}$. Since CDEF is a square. We have:

$$\overline{DE}^2 = \overline{AD} \times \overline{FB} = (2 - \overline{CD}) \times (3 - \overline{CF}) = 6 - 5 \times \overline{DE} + \overline{DE}^2$$

So, $5 \times \overline{DE} = 6, \overline{DE} = 1.2$

The answer is [B].

Other similar problems

AMC 8 2019 problem 24

AMC 8 2023 problem 19

Geometry is a big topic. So it is not surprising that we meet one or several geometry problems in the AMC 8 exam. Geometry includes not only those we just discussed but also many other knowledge points. Don't forget, we also need to learn some basic knowledge of three-dimensional shapes.

Problem #36

Given that the star has area 5.6, what is the volume of the prism?

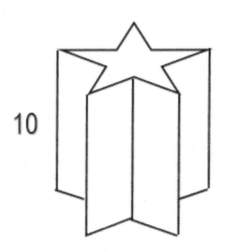

10

(A) 49   (B) 56   (C) 64   (D) 81   (E) 100

Solution

Volume of prisms can be calculated by multiplying the base and height.

$5.6 \times 10 = 56$

Answer is [B]

Other similar problems

AMC 8 2022 problem 24

AMC 8 2023 problem 17

Keep Learning

I add this section, but not because adults always intend to make kids study hard. As you may have noticed already, in the geometry section, we did not go over all geometric knowledge points. There are many many math knowledge points that we are not able to cover in this book. You need to keep learning. Some of these AMC 8 questions are basic, but use some math terms, and never give explanation. So please go ahead to learn more, and prepare for the exam.

— END —

Made in United States
Orlando, FL
28 September 2024

52047149R00046